M000015165

THE CHICAGO BOARD OF TRADE BUILDING

A BUILDING BOOK FROM THE CHICAGO ARCHITECTURE FOUNDATION

EDWARD KEEGAN

Pomegranate

SAN FRANCISCO

Published by Pomegranate Communications, Inc.
Box 808022, Petaluma CA 94975
800 227 1428; www.pomegranate.com

Pomegranate Europe Ltd.
Unit 1, Heathcote Business Centre, Hurlbutt Road
Warwick, Warwickshire CV34 6TD, UK
[+44] 0 1926 430111; sales@pomeurope.co.uk

Library of Congress Control Number: 2005905018

ISBN 0-7649-3505-4
Pomegranate Catalog No. A105

Cover and book design by Lynn Bell, Monroe Street Studios, Santa Rosa CA

Printed in Korea

14 13 12 11 10 09 08 07 06 05   10 9 8 7 6 5 4 3 2 1

Mission

The Chicago Architecture Foundation (CAF) is dedicated to advancing public interest and education in architecture and related design. CAF pursues this mission through a comprehensive program of tours, lectures, exhibitions, special programs, and youth programs, all designed to enhance the public's awareness and appreciation of Chicago's important architectural legacy.

Founded in 1966, the Chicago Architecture Foundation has evolved to become a nationally recognized resource advancing public interest and education in Chicago's outstanding architecture. Its programs serve more than 250,000 people each year. For more information, contact us at the address below, or visit us on our website:

Chicago Architecture Foundation
224 South Michigan Avenue
Chicago IL 60604
312-922-TOUR (8687)
www.architecture.org

In celebration of the Chicago Board of Trade Building's seventy-fifth anniversary, we are pleased to introduce this book as the latest addition to a series of building monographs. The effort of putting together this book was a collaboration of many people with an interest in Chicago's built environment and the mission of the Chicago Architecture Foundation.

Our gratitude to the Chicago Board of Trade Building, Chairman Charles P. Carey, President and CEO Bernard W. Dan, and V.P. of Real Estate Operations Kevin Lennon, who made this book possible by opening up their archive of photographs.

At UIC Daley Library Special Collections Department, thanks to Owen Gregory, who maintains the Chicago Board of Trade Archives.

At Hedrich Blessing, our gratitude to Scott Brennan and Bob Shimer, for opening up their archive of recent images to us.

To Mark Segal, our thanks for working with us to find the right cover image.

We would also like to acknowledge the work of CAF's in-house staff and freelancers, who conceived, assembled, and promoted this book. They include Ned Cramer, curator; Stacy Koumbis, director of operations; Billy Shelton, merchandise manager; Edward Keegan, author; Iris Blumenthal, copy reader; and Beth Treacy, marketing consultant.

—Lynn J. Osmond, President and CEO
Chicago Architecture Foundation

Chronology

1837   The City of Chicago is incorporated.

1848   The Chicago Board of Trade is established to facilitate the trading of grain and other agricultural products.

1885   The Board of Trade moves into its W. W. Boyington–designed building at the foot of LaSalle Street on Jackson Boulevard. Its 300-foot-tall tower is the city's highest structure.

1930   The 1885 building is replaced by the present structure, a 609-foot-tall Art Deco design by Holabird & Root. Once again, the Board of Trade occupies the city's tallest building.

1975   The 57-foot-tall trading room is divided into two spaces to meet the growing demands of the Board of Trade.

1982   A new annex designed by Murphy/Jahn is constructed to the south of the 1930 building. The primary trading activities are moved to the new structure.

1997   Fujikawa Johnson & Associates designs a new addition that spans LaSalle Street and adds a new trading floor at the corner of Clark and Van Buren Streets. This building has the capability of being doubled in height on its foundations if additional space is needed in the future.

2005   The Holabird & Root–designed building celebrates its seventy-fifth anniversary. Statues from the 1885 building return to the Chicago Board of Trade as part of a renovated plaza to the east of the 1930 building.

At 10 AM on June 9, 1930, President Herbert Hoover touched a golden telegraph key in Washington, DC, and set trading in motion at the new forty-five-story limestone home of the Board of Trade in Chicago. The new building had risen over the preceding eighteen months on a site at the intersection of LaSalle Street and Jackson Boulevard, home to the Board since 1885.

Members and dignitaries gathered earlier that morning at the Board's temporary home at Clark and Van Buren Streets and marched in a short parade to the new structure. There, a reported fifty thousand to one hundred thousand interested citizens joined them for the opening ceremonies led by Board president John A. Bunnell. Officials had intended to clear the floor prior to the start of trading, but the crush of the crowd was so great that the day became an intriguing spectacle in which the general public mingled with traders on the floor during the frenetic transaction of business.

The dedication came less than eight months after the crash of world financial markets had sparked the Great Depression, hardly an auspicious time to inaugurate a dazzling new tower dedicated to commerce in America's heartland. Designed by local architects John A. Holabird and John Wellborn Root Jr., the highly articulated and carefully incised limestone masses climbed toward the sky in a series of artfully configured setbacks to a pyramidal roof where an aluminum statue of Ceres would soon bring the building to a total height of 609 feet. This celebrated silhouette would remain the tallest building in Chicago for the next quarter of a century.

"Here it stands, completed, the new Board of Trade building, monarch
of LaSalle Street, towering head and shoulders above its mighty neighbors, commanding focal point of Chicago's financial heart."—The opening lines from the souvenir program given at the building's dedication.

The Chicago Board of Trade has been a central institution within the city's economic fabric since the Board's inception in 1848, a scant eleven years after the incorporation of the city itself. Chicago's own growth was predicated on its convenient location near natural waterways. In 1847, the Illinois and Michigan Canal completed these connections; this crucial waterway linked the Great Lakes with the mid-continental highway of the Mississippi River, allowing unfettered waterborne traffic between the East and the great breadbasket of the Midwest. Chicago consolidated its advantages by installing telegraph communications the same year. A great network of transcontinental railroads continued to grow in the following decades, with the city as its central hub.

Prior to 1848, because no centralized trading market existed for grain, farmers brought their produce to Chicago during harvest season for sale to those who could transport it to other parts of the nation. To search for the best price they could find, they were forced to carry their harvest from merchant to merchant. Barges and wagons filled with grain congested the city's streets and waterways, and some unsuccessful sellers had been known to dump their grain into the lake when oversupply failed to produce buyers. The inefficiencies in this scattered "system" led to drastic price fluctuations, to the detriment of buyers and sellers. There was no fixed standard for quality of products; even the weight per bushel varied for each transaction.

The Chicago Board of Trade created an efficient market that solved these problems, and it grew as rapidly as did the city. Its first quarters were in a room above the Gage and Haines flour store at 101 South Water Street. Renting space as necessary within the central business district, the Board moved six times before the end of the Civil War. In 1865, the Board moved into a two-story space within the Chamber of Commerce Building at LaSalle and Washington Streets and stayed there until the structure was destroyed in the Chicago Fire of 1871. The Board temporarily relocated to a fanciful structure known as the Wigwam while the Chamber of Commerce was rebuilt. In 1881, the Board purchased a piece of property on Jackson Boulevard at the foot of LaSalle Street, which would become its permanent home.

W. W. Boyington, famed as the designer of the Chicago Water Tower, was commissioned to design the Board's first purpose-built home on its current site. His eclectic ten-story design, constructed of granite and topped by a 300-foot tower, became the city's tallest structure at the time. The building—the first commercial building in Chicago to feature electric lighting—was dedicated on April 29, 1885. With various modifications, the Boyington structure served as the Chicago Board of Trade's home for the next forty-three years.

An early rendering of the 1885 W. W. Boyington—
designed Chicago Board of Trade shows its eclecticism.

Kaufmann and Fabry Co.

The 1885 building's central tower, once 300 feet tall, was removed early in the twentieth century. This undated photograph was taken during the 1920s, shortly before the building's demolition. Note the matching classical temple fronts of the Federal Reserve Bank (at right) and Illinois Merchants Bank (at left), which still frame the Board of Trade.

By the 1920s, Holabird & Roche was in its fifth decade of professional practice. When the Chicago Board of Trade initially employed the firm in 1909, it was recognized as the most established and technically proficient firm in the city. William A. Holabird and Martin Roche had trained together in the firm of William Le Baron Jenney, an early career stop for many luminaries, including Daniel Burnham and Louis Sullivan. Not only had Holabird & Roche designed some of the most historically important buildings—the 1889 Tacoma Building, the 1894 Marquette Building, and the Old Colony Building of the same year—but in 1909 the firm was also busy designing and constructing the imposing civic block that still houses the city's government, the Chicago City Hall–County Building.

Holabird & Root, the successor firm to Holabird & Roche, was named for its second generation of Chicago architect principals. John A. Holabird was son of firm founder William A. Holabird. The father of John Wellborn Root Jr. was Daniel Burnham's legendary partner, who designed the seminal Chicago landmarks the Rookery and the Monadnock Building before his untimely death in 1891. The sons had become friends before the First World War while students at the École des Beaux-Arts in Paris; in 1919 they became principals of Holabird & Roche. The firm name remained until 1928, when, following the death of both its founders earlier in the decade, it was changed to Holabird & Root. Both Holabird and Root followed their fathers' professional specializations; Holabird was primarily responsible for management (the firm numbered over two hundred employees during the mid-1920s as the Board of Trade Building design came into existence), and Root was the principal designer.

When the firm finally geared up for the design and construction of the Chicago Board of Trade Building in 1927, its work was evolving to help define the new Art Deco style. One clear local influence was the highly acclaimed second-place entry by Finnish architect Eliel Saarinen for the Chicago Tribune Tower in 1922. Although Holabird & Roche claimed third place in that important competition, the firm's designs increasingly followed Saarinen's spare and abstract vertical piers and planes in works such as the slim 333 North Michigan Avenue and the carefully sculpted setbacks of the Palmolive Building.

THE DESIGN PROCESS

Holabird & Roche first prepared designs for the Chicago Board of Trade in 1909, when the firm assigned it project number 877, a designation that would identify the drawings for more than two decades of work. The firm appears to have worked initially only on a remodeling of the 1885 building, but by 1912 it had been asked to prepare plans for a new building.

Finnish architect Eliel Saarinen's second-place entry in the 1922 Chicago Tribune Tower Competition was influential for years afterward, inspiring architects to experiment with strong vertical expressions of windows, stepped setbacks, and abstract ornament to create a bold new look for tall buildings.

Chicago Tribune

Holabird & Roche captured third place in the Tribune Tower Competition
with a tower design that combined both classical and Gothic details.

At least one fifteen- or sixteen-story scheme was produced during the period, although the drawings for that proposal have never been found. By 1925, a series of developments made a new building even more likely. The W. W. Boyington structure of 1885, then housing the Board of Trade, had newer and more imposing neighbors to the north across Jackson Boulevard. On the west side of LaSalle Street, a 1922 design by Graham, Anderson, Probst & White housed the Chicago branch of the Federal Reserve Bank. The same firm, a successor to that of architect Daniel H. Burnham, also designed a home for the Illinois Merchants Bank (later the Continental Illinois Bank) on the east side of the street in 1924. These two staid limestone structures filled their respective blocks, and their paired classical entrance porticos framed the southern end of LaSalle Street in a monumental manner that spoke of the great dignity and sobriety of their business affairs. Boyington's forty-year-old design, a hodge-podge of design motifs typical of its era, had lost its commanding tower some years earlier to the building's uneven settlement on Chicago's sandy soils. Between these imposing new edifices, it looked woefully inadequate.

Both neighboring structures illustrate the predominant office-building type of the time in Chicago—260 or so feet high, with exterior walls rising straight up from the sidewalks on all four sides. These massive structures offered significantly more interior space than the Boyington building did, but changes in Chicago's zoning law opened new design opportunities and, not inconsiderably, a potential envelope that could create large quantities of rentable office space on the existing site. A 1923 zoning revision allowed towers covering up to 25 percent of the site above 260 feet; this change encouraged a new form of tower that would culminate with the present Chicago Board of Trade's distinctive massing.

In early 1925, Holabird & Roche's continuing role as the Board of Trade's architect came under attack. It is not clear which Holabird & Roche design elicited the opening salvo, but a February 10 letter from Chicago architect Alfred Granger to Henry Rumsey, chairman of the Board of Trade's New Building Committee, was an amalgam of architectural critique, civic pride, and naked opportunism. He lambasted Holabird's design, citing what he melodramatically characterized as the "universal criticism of architects all over the world." Referring to a detail wherein heavy columns were to be placed above street-level glazing, Granger twisted his rhetorical knife, describing it as "just about as bad architecture as can be invented."

Granger cloaked his intentions to secure the commission by presenting himself as "a representative of the profession in Chicago" whose civic-minded activities were meant for the betterment of the city. He signed his letter as president of the Chicago chapter, American Institute of Architects, but disingenuously sent it under the letterhead of his firm, Granger, Lowe & Bollenbacher Architects.

Within a week, Holabird and Roche wrote to Rumsey, detailing their long-term relationship with the Board of Trade, but made no specific mention of

Granger's letter. "Since 1916," they wrote, "a part of every year has been given in our office to study and sketches in preparation of the time we would be requested to proceed with our work." They clearly indicated that they had no interest in allowing an interloper to suddenly walk away with the prestigious commission. The letter speaks of the opportunities that the recent zoning changes presented. In words prophetic of the newly evolving Art Deco towers that would soon rise, the letter stated, "This ordinance stimulates character in design and offers many opportunities for individual expression in building impossible under the former ordinance."

Rumsey quickly responded that as the new chairman of the Building Committee he was still trying to determine the status of Holabird's 1916 contract. While cordial and deferential, Rumsey was clearly open to other firms' interest in the project.

The remainder of that year and the following year saw great efforts by the New Building Committee in exploring options for another structure. At least six serious proposals, some including architectural designs, were developed during this period. The chief participants included a team led by Marshall Field, with a design by Graham, Anderson, Probst & White; architect Alfred S. Alschuler; architects D. H. Burnham & Company, led by Daniel H. Burnham Jr.; McLennan Construction, with a design by the New York firm of Warren & Wetmore, architects of that city's Grand Central Terminal; the scheming Chicago architect Alfred Granger; and long-term Chicago Board of Trade architects Holabird & Roche.

The complexities of the variations the building committee considered from 1925 to 1926 make it difficult to reconstruct the deliberations or even to assess all the factors considered. On March 11, 1927, the committee sent letters of regret to all but one of the aforementioned teams, announcing that Holabird & Roche had been formally chosen as architect of the new building. More than twenty-four months after Alfred Granger initially questioned the firm's design competence, the Chicago Board of Trade reaffirmed its architect of eighteen years.

THE BUILDING SITE

The Chicago Board of Trade Building sits on the most dramatic building site within the city's central business district. The Chicago ground plan is simple and democratic—a gridiron of blocks 320 feet square, each equal in size and as important as the next. But a shift in the grid at Jackson and LaSalle Streets produced the rare Chicago site where a building could sit within the city plan and have an axial relationship to the street it fronts. Since its purchase of that property in 1885, the Board of Trade has held this dominant location on LaSalle Street. The Board's historic role as a central player to the city's economic community is perfectly reflected in its locale; we have here a serendipitous merger of form and function.

Holabird and Roche recognized this when they described their design in October 1927:

> In the exterior, we have attempted to express the various functions of the building and to erect a structure essentially modern in character, majestic in its dignity and size, a landmark at the foot of LaSalle Street, dominant in its unchanging beauty in the financial district and a fitting and permanent manifestation of the traditions of the Board of Trade.

The building's art is conceived as a narrative specific to the Board of Trade:

> Sculpted figures accentuate the receding planes and angles of the building, and the story surrounding the activities within the building is clearly told in the symbolic ornamental carvings.

Building Massing and Organization

Holabird & Root designed three distinct floor plans that shape the Board of Trade's massing and setbacks. The base fills the block bounded by Jackson Boulevard on the north, LaSalle Street on the east, Sherman Street (now Financial Place) on the west, and, originally, an alley on the south. A three-story-tall lobby, called the arcade, sits at roughly the center of the block, with the elevators situated toward the southern end of the structure. The upper portion of the nine-story base was occupied primarily by the trading room, an open space 164 feet long by 113 feet wide, a 57-foot ceiling, and full-height windows facing north along Jackson Boulevard. Because of the trading floor's large size, few individual rooms on the lower floors were very far from the exterior wall's windows—a key design constraint before air-conditioning became a widespread feature of buildings.

The middle section of the building, extending from the ninth to the twenty-third floor, is U shaped, with an open light well facing north. This follows one of the prevalent layouts for office floor plans in Chicago between the 1880s and 1920s, when almost every building was either a solid block with a central light well (like the Rookery or the Railway Exchange Building) or a U-shaped configuration (such as the Marquette Building). The one distinction between the Chicago Board of Trade and its local precedents is the placement of its mass on the site. The earlier examples always deployed the solid face of their mass toward the main street and faced the open court of the U toward the alley. This configuration is inverted in the Board of Trade: the open end is toward the front of the structure on Jackson Street; here it continues the canyon effect of LaSalle Street and enhances the drama of the tower at the rear of the site.

The upper floors are the tower itself, covering only 25 percent of the block per the new zoning regulations. Deftly integrated by Holabird's designers, the tower seems to grow naturally from the rear mass of the building's midsection. Subtle setbacks and indentations simultaneously break down the overall mass and accentuate the verticality of the structure.

The three different floor plans are each highly efficient for varying spaces that are necessary within the structure. The base permitted the large expanse of the trading room; the midsection suited larger firms that wished to have their offices in continuous spaces while maintaining close proximity to the outside walls for light and ventilation; and the tower worked best when subdivided into small offices and suites, perfect for many trading firms that were individuals or small groups of partners. While the economics of the tall office building has changed a great deal in the seventy-five years since the Board of Trade Building was completed, this rich mix of different spaces still serves a variety of tenants well.

A single elevator rises to the forty-third floor, where a final flight of stairs reaches the uppermost occupied floor. When the building opened, the forty-fourth floor featured the city's premier observation platform. The outlook sat at the base of the pyramidal roof structure, public space wrapped all four sides of the building, and the sloped glass exterior walls had operable windows. The observation deck was open long after it had been supplanted as the city's tallest, but with nearby Sears Tower more than twice as tall and the inevitable leaks that occur with forty-year-old glazing, the deck was closed in

the early 1970s, and its glass was replaced
with metal roofing. The once-dramatic
space is now a dark and attic-like area,
although several roof hatches open to still
spectacular views of the city.

DESIGN DEVELOPMENT, CONSTRUCTION, AND INTERIORS

Holabird's staff prepared many schemes during the period from the firm's con-
firmation as building architects in early 1927 through the building's completion in 1930. Although the evolution of the design was never clearly detailed
by the architects, the overall organization as described above remained rela-
tively constant.

An image that defined the building's place in architectural history was initially released in 1928. Drawn by acclaimed architectural illustrator Hugh
Ferris, the charcoal rendering depicts the Chicago Board of Trade as the soar-
ing punctuation for the LaSalle Street canyon.

After the Board of Trade vacated its 1885 home, wrecking commenced on
December 7, 1928. A press release that day revealed that the completed building and land would be valued at over $20 million; the exterior would be clad
in Indiana limestone, surmounted by an observatory 525 feet above the

Famed architectural renderer Hugh Ferris produced this classic image of the Chicago Board of Trade Building in 1927. This early version of the design included large classical columns that framed the trading room windows.

street, with the top of the statue bringing it
to 600 feet.

Bids for the new building were received
that same month, and the Hegeman-Harris
Company was selected as general contrac-
tor soon after. The company's previous
structures in Chicago included the Chicago
Tribune Tower and Holabird's earlier
designs for 333 North Michigan Avenue
and the Chicago Daily News. Demolition was completed in less than three
months, and new construction began on February 28, 1929, with details of the
final design still under consideration by the architects and the client.

Construction continued through 1929 at a brisk pace. Occasionally the
client indicated concern about the construction schedule, particularly when
the booming economy created a shortage of workers on the site, but contrac-
tors Hegeman-Harris persevered while Holabird & Root assuaged the concerns
of the Board of Trade. The stock market crash of October 1929 passed without
mention in the minutes of the weekly construction meetings.

As the building neared completion, Holabird & Root provided a written
description of the public areas on the lower levels of the new building:

> In this arcade will be found an expression indicative of the progressive
> spirit associated with the great mart known as the Board of Trade. . . .

This construction photograph shows the erection of immense 227-ton trusses that span the trading floor and support the office structure.

Chicago Architectural Photographing Company

As the steel is erected for the tower in the rear, exterior
stonework already clads the first twelve floors.

This late-construction photograph shows the corner of Jackson Boulevard and LaSalle Street not significantly different from what it is today. Holabird & Root's designers carefully articulated the east wall of the trading room with shallow stone insets that match the north-facing windows in size and proportion. The clock has yet to be set within its completed sculptural surround.

The top of the building is highly articulated with a series of dramatic
setbacks crowned by the pyramid and statue of Ceres. In this view,
the observatory glazing is clearly seen at the base of the pyramid.

At each end of the arcade will be found a lighting system unique in the impressive vertical shafts of illuminated glass running from floor to ceiling and joining at the ceiling with a burnished metal reflector, which will cast a silvery light over the entire area of the arcade.

It was in the arcade and the surrounding lobby spaces where Holabird & Root's designers made their most distilled statement about architecture, urbanity, and the Chicago Board of Trade. The arcade and lobby were carefully planned as an interior microcosm of the city itself; doors led from the arcade and adjacent elevators to all four adjoining streets. The three-story arcade's height was a result of the building's internal organization: the floor of the original trading room is directly above that ceiling. A symphony of luxurious and durable stone, set against elegant nickel silver metalwork, plays throughout these public spaces. Restaurants and shops provide services to workers and visitors alike. The arcade's three-story-high piers create miniature skyscrapers, with cascades of contrasting stone providing metaphoric clouds in this carefully choreographed landscape. Even today, it is difficult to escape the exuberant optimism at the heart of the entire building.

The fourth floor featured the building's raison d'être—the trading room. Occupying the entire north half of the structure, it measured 113 by 164 feet, with a ceiling height of 57 feet. To accommodate this space without need of interior supports, six trusses, each 227 tons, spanned its ceiling. Much of the trading room floor was devoted to large octagonal pits, one each for wheat, corn, oats,

Touted as the world's largest light fixture at the building's opening, the central fixture runs the length of the arcade's ceiling and continues down the walls to the second-floor balcony.

The three-story arcade was designed as a miniature city skyline, with tall
piers resembling skyscrapers that are separated by abstract billowing clouds.

BOARD OF TRADE
CIGAR SHOP
TEMPORARY LOCATION

Chesterfield
Light one for me!

POST OFFICE NEWS
BOOK SHOP
RENTAL LIBRARY

$1
EVERY
ANY BOOK
IN THIS WINDOW

Chicago Board of Trade

Lobby storefronts, elegant essays in Art Deco composition,
reflected the favored vertical direction of the designer.

Subtle changes over the years to the lobby, still as stunning in the early twenty-first century as it was in 1930, include the addition of circular downlights to both sides of the ceiling light fixture and wall sconces on each pier that echo the cloudlike forms of the original soffits.

These light fixtures, now being restored as part of the seventy-fifth anniversary renovations, originally illuminated the low space between the front door and the arcade.

rye, cotton, and provisions. The north side of the room, with floor-to-ceiling windows that provided an even, indirect natural light, was the location for some thirty-six grain tables, which were used to inspect samples of the produce being traded in the adjacent pits. A large portion of the room was paneled in English oak, with nickel grilles as decorative accents, and the other three walls were devoid of windows. A balcony at the building's fifth-floor level wrapped the east, south, and west walls, providing a small area for a visitors' gallery and allowing easy access to the constantly updated chalkboards, the method used to display prices before the development of electronic devices decades later.

A second large trading floor occupied the southeast corner of the fourth floor. Architectural plans indicate the room's intended use by the Chicago Stock Exchange, although that group never became a tenant, and the space was used as the securities trading room, an early expansion of the Board's original trade in commodities that spurred much of the institution's expansion late in the twentieth century.

ORNAMENTATION

John Storrs' aluminum statue of Ceres crowned the building's pyramidal roof 609 feet above the sidewalk. The American-born sculptor designed the piece in his Paris studio to depict the traditional Roman goddess of agriculture, in whose honor grain foods are called "cereals." The 31-foot-high piece weighed 6,500 pounds and was cast by the Bronze Division of The Gorham Company in Providence, Rhode Island, from a special aluminum alloy made for architectural applications by Apex Smelting Company of Chicago. Storrs described his composition shortly before its installation:

> The vertical lines of the building itself are retained in the lines of the statue. Because of the great height at which it will stand, the matter of

The original 57-foot-tall trading room on the fourth floor was the heart of the Chicago Board of Trade Building. The octagonal trading pits were in the center of the floor, with the grain tables for inspection of produce to the right, under the windows, along the north wall. The balcony on the fifth floor (left side of the photograph) was the visitors' gallery, and chalkboards for constantly updated price quotations were on the same level, along the far wall.

detail did not have to be taken into consideration. The outline of a woman's figure is suggested rather than rendered exactly.

The intricate light fixture, 38 feet across and weighing 8 tons, was suspended in the center of the trading room and mirrored the octagonal shape of the trading pits on the floor.

A continuous horizontal chalkboard on the balcony level conveyed current pricing
information to all on the trading room floor. Tall nickel metal grilles continued the
pattern of the windows on the north wall to the other walls enclosing the space.

Ceres holds a sheaf of wheat in her left hand and in her right hand, a sample bag of grain, not unlike those goods examined by traders under the light of
the Jackson Boulevard windows.

Surrounded by miniature prosceniums that make the entrance to the building a theatrical experience, the front doors are set back from the sidewalk.

Grain forms the basis for the decorative motifs above the
main doors inside the Jackson Boulevard entrances.

After Ceres, the most notable sculpture on the exterior is the trio of figures

that surrounds the clock on the ninth-floor roof level. Not just a functional

timepiece, this limestone slab shields a series of rooftop exhaust vents from

the trading room below. Sculptor Alvin Meyer provided the following explana-

tion for his work:

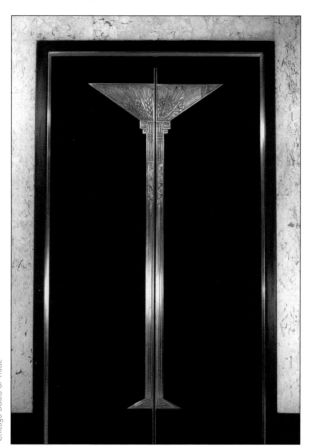

A decorative motif on the first-floor elevator doors displays
a sheaf of wheat that, at the top, fans across both doors.

The third-floor elevator doors feature a woven abstract metal pattern.

On the fourth floor—location of the trading room—
different ornamental patterns grace each elevator door.

Nickel silver gates protected the entrance to the trading floor. Each opening featured four sculptural panels that depicted scenes from the city and the Chicago Board of Trade's history.

Denoting its importance as the home of the trading room, the fourth-floor elevator lobby is finished completely in stone.

The idea in mind regarding the clock group on the front of the Board of Trade Building is to symbolize the birth of wheat and corn.

As far as we know, wheat was the chief grain of the early inhabitants of Mesopotamia. The Chaldeans and their ancestors already used wheat as a motif in their works of art, probably as early as 2500 B.C. The figure holding

Chicago Board of Trade

The second-floor (above) and the
third-floor (left) elevator lobbies
have unusual geometrically
inspired terrazzo floor patterns.

Chicago Board of Trade

John Storrs' stylized statue of Ceres crowns the building. The folds in the goddess' robes continue the vertical emphasis of the building's design. Three details are worth noting: Ceres holds a bag of grain in her right hand; in her left hand she holds a sheaf of wheat; and not readily apparent from 609 feet below on the street, her face is blank.

Chicago Board of Trade

Three figures guard the clock on the building's front facade: a native
of Mesopotamia holding a sheaf of wheat (left); an American
eagle (above); and a Native American with maize (right).

the wheat is to represent not a Babylonian warrior, but a peaceful citizen of
an early time who, historically at least, gave us wheat.

The opposite figure holding corn is an American Indian, also not a warrior, but an agricultural one. What we know as corn is the Indian maize,

for the European corn of our ancestors is distinctly different. Therefore, historically, our corn was brought to us by the red man.

In the center appears an eagle, emblematic of the spirit of America guarding our agricultural interests.

THE COMPLETION

A milestone was reached on April 5, 1930, when the Quaker Oats Company moved in as the building's first tenant. The Building Committee reported that the structure was substantially complete on May 1, 1930, five weeks before the official dedication on June 9, 1930.

When the Chicago Board of Trade Building was topped out with its sculpture of Ceres later that year, the building became the first structure in Chicago to break the 600-foot height. Although known as the birthplace of the skyscraper, Chicago, with its more restrictive zoning, had long since given up the contest to New York, which had eclipsed this height twenty-two years earlier. At that time, the 612-foot Singer Tower in Manhattan had set the standard.

On November 18, 1931, almost eighteen months after the building's dedication and a decade and a half after its inception, the directors of the Board of Trade officially discharged the New Building Committee, effectively ending the process that brought their stunning new headquarters into existence.

CHANGES

As a working office building, the Chicago Board of Trade Building has endured changes, both large and small, since its original occupancy in 1930. The introduction of new technologies, the developing needs of traders, and even the evolving interest in historic preservation have all shaped the Board of Trade Building into the complex that exists today.

In 1971, Chicago-based mechanical engineers ESD carried out significant changes in upgrading mechanical systems. Rooftop penthouses, metal-clad structures that subtly alter

Sketches provide a partial explanation of the intricate choreography that the open outcry system utilizes.

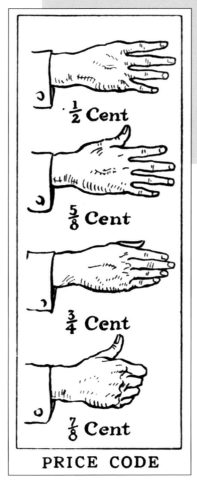

Chicago Board of Trade

In the cash grain section of the floor, Liebenow and Crabtree look over a state-graded sample of corn, while George F. Sheeren (of Louis Dreyfus Corporation), representative of an exporter, informs the home office of his purchases.

Holabird & Root's original massing, were added on the twenty-fourth floor facing LaSalle Street.

The 1930 building's most significant remodeling occurred in 1975, when Alfred Shaw & Associates split the trading room vertically, creating two separate trading spaces and doubling the floor area. Although many of the original fixtures and furnishings had been removed over the previous four decades, this revision destroyed what original character remained of the room. Construction of the new decking was done at night and on weekends, but the need to install temporary shoring for long-span trusses in the main room led to awkward conditions that gave the generally frenetic activities in the pits the touch of a construction carnival. Many photographs from this period depict traders at work in their signature colored jackets topped by hard hats.

In 1977, the city of Chicago granted landmark designation to portions of the building, specifically most of the Jackson Boulevard facade and parts of the interior lobby and balconies.

That same year, the Board finally acquired the property to its south, between the 1930 building and Van Buren Street. This had been the site of the old Postal Telegraph Building and was the subject of design proposals during deliberations of the Building Committee in the mid-1920s. Murphy/Jahn, led by the firm's young

The forty-fourth-floor
observatory was a destina-
tion for Chicagoans from
the building's opening
until nearby Sears Tower
was constructed in the
early 1970s.

Photograph © Hedrich Blessing

The division of the trading
room into two levels in 1975
required that temporary
columns be placed within the
space; many traders wore hard
hats during this period.

Photograph © Hedrich Blessing

designer Helmut Jahn, proposed a silver and black-glass–clad structure that reinterpreted many of Holabird & Root's setbacks in a more contemporary manner.

"The new building relates formally and visually to special ornamental features
of the older one; the shape of the roof, an ornament at the top, the setbacks and
the spandrels," Jahn explained at the time. "We repeat the whole vertical character of the original." The new rooftop ornament is considerably simpler than
John Storrs' Ceres—an abstracted octagon that represents the ubiquitous pits
where the Board's traders continue to operate under the open outcry system.
The new trading floor, housing the agriculture and grain pits that were the
Board's original endeavors, was located on the fourth floor, with considerably
more technology packed into its large volume. Above, Jahn created an interior
atrium ringed with offices, each of which enjoyed natural daylight from two
directions. The north wall of Jahn's glassy atrium is the old masonry facade of
the 1930 building, a compelling combination of new and old. John Norton's
painting of Ceres, which had been removed from the old trading room when it
was split more than a decade earlier, was reinstalled in the new atrium.

Soon after Jahn's addition, the rapid expansion of the Board's financial
trading markets created a need for a new trading floor. Chicago-based
Fujikawa Johnson & Associates, a successor firm to that of the legendary
Ludwig Mies van der Rohe, created a bulky long-span structure directly to the
east of Jahn's earlier addition. This new building, some 215 feet by 245 feet,
features clear spans for its full width. Its foundations are capable of support-
ing a future trading floor above. A 50-foot-wide bridge, eleven stories in

Murphy/Jahn

Murphy/Jahn's glass-clad addition reinterpreted the notches and setbacks
of the original building in a manner popular during the early 1980s.

Murphy/Jahn crowned the pyramidal roof of the new annex with an octagon—
symbolic of the trading pits—reminiscent of John Storrs' Ceres half a century earlier.

Murphy/Jahn

The upper floors of the Murphy/Jahn addition surround an atrium that faces the
south facade of the Holabird & Root tower. John Norton's 35-foot-tall mural
of Ceres, which had adorned the trading room from 1930 until its renovation
in 1975, found a new home supported by a trellis structure within the atrium.

Murphy/Jahn's lobby provided a new entrance from Van Buren
Street. The forms of the balcony and the long light fixture in
the ceiling owe a debt of inspiration to the original building.

height, attaches the buildings across LaSalle Street and results in the current L-
shaped configuration of the entire complex. The covered drive beneath the
new structure, while hardly the aesthetic triumph of the 1930 building, was a
welcome respite from Chicago's extremes of weather during the year.

Fujikawa Johnson's 1997 addition lies to the east of Murphy/Jahn's earlier addition.

Even as the 1930 building celebrates its seventy-fifth anniversary in 2005,
change remains an ongoing project at the Chicago Board of Trade. The exterior
masonry has been cleaned and is receiving restoration where required under
the guidance of Austin AECOM. Two ornamental statues that long graced the
facade of W. W. Boyington's 1885 building are also returning to LaSalle and
Jackson as part of the year's seventy-fifth anniversary festivities. The 12-foot
tall, 5-ton granite goddesses representing agriculture and industry were
apparently salvaged by Board grain trader Arthur Cutten, who moved them to
his Glen Ellyn, Illinois, estate, where local officials discovered them when they
acquired the property in 1978. Since then, they have presided over a Wheaton
parking lot, but DuPage County Forest Preserve District commissioners donated
them to the Chicago Board of Trade after learning of their downtown origins.
The statues recall that the Chicago Board of Trade has stood, in two different
buildings, at the foot of LaSalle Street for 120 years. While the frenetic trading
of the pits has moved to newer contiguous structures to the south, the 1930
building's dramatic silhouette capped by Ceres is still an essential part of the
Chicago skyline. Although the Chicago Board of Trade is hundreds of feet
shorter than many of its newer neighbors, its distinctive design continues to
make the building "the monarch of LaSalle Street."

Chicago Board of Trade

Two statues that long adorned the
entrance to the 1885 W. W.
Boyington–designed building have been
relocated to LaSalle Street, as part of
the festivities celebrating the seventy-
fifth anniversary of the 1930 building.

Chicago Board of Trade

The Chicago Board of Trade provides a suitable background
for a ticker-tape parade on LaSalle Street (circa 1961).